劳工节

Customs, Traditions and Landmarks |
Non-Fiction Series

Copyright © 2022 by Level Learning, INC. and Washington Yu Ying PCS™
Original and Edited Text Copyright © 2022 by Washington Yu Ying PCS™

All rights reserved. No part of this book in whole or part may be reproduced without written permission from the publisher.

Published by Level Learning

Content Contributors:
Washington Yu Ying PCS™
Level Learning - Ya-Ching Chang

Illustrations by: Josh Taira

Leveling classification based on Level Learning standard. For full description, visit www.levellearning.com

ISBN 978-1-64040-015-3
Simplified Chinese Edition

About Level Learning:

Level Learning provides a literacy focused curriculum specifically designed for K-12 Chinese as a Second Language classrooms. Our program offers 20 levels of specific and detailed objectives, leveled texts and passages, mastery-based online assessment, and analytics to enable data-driven instruction. Level Learning reading curriculum for both literature and informational text emphasize grammar and comprehension skills to help teachers develop confident and independent Chinese language readers. The non-fiction series of books are specifically designed to support our informational text course based on multiple national standards. To learn more about our entire offering, visit www.levellearning.com.

About Washington Yu Ying PCS™:

Washington Yu Ying PCS is a Mandarin English dual language immersion International Baccalaureate (IB) World school. Yu Ying's mission is to inspire and prepare young people to create a better world by challenging them to reach their full potential in a nurturing Chinese/English educational environment. Yu Ying's comprehensive IB, dual immersion curriculum equips students with global competencies for success in the real world. As a leader in immersion education, Yu Ying is determined to advance Chinese language programs and global citizenry education by helping other schools create and strengthen their Chinese programs. For more information, email: products@washingtonyuying.org

	九月					
星期一	星期二	星期三	星期四	星期五	星期六	星期日
	1	2	3	4	5	6
7	8	9	10	11	12	13
14	15	16	17	18	19	20
21	22	23	24	25	26	27
28	29	30				

每年九月的第一个星期一,是美国的劳工节。

在劳工节假期，很多人不用去工作，学生们也不用去上学。

为什么美国有劳工节假期呢?

1882年9月5日，纽约市有一群工人上街游行。这群工人希望有更多的休息时间。他们也希望得到更多收入。

那时候的工人,工作时间很长,收入却很少。

后来，每年九月的第一个星期，纽约市的工人都会上街游行。其他地方的工人知道了，也都上街游行。他们的希望被大家听到了。

在1894年，美国把每年九月的第一个星期一定为劳工节。多年以后，工人一星期只要工作四十个小时。因此，工人们有了更多的时间休息，也得到了更多的收入。

有了劳工节假期，大家也有时间做不同的活动。有些人会去旅行，有些人会看球赛。

你的劳工节假期会做什么呢?

Glossary

	Pinyin	English Definition
劳工节	láo gōng jié	Labor Day
假期	jià qī	holiday
纽约市	niǔ yuē shì	New York City
一群	yì qún	a group
上街游行	shàng jiē yóu xíng	street parade
希望	xī wàng	to hope
更多	gèng duō	more
收入	shōu rù	income
却	què	but
其他	qí tā	other
听到	tīng dào	to hear
定为	dìng wéi	set, establish
小时	xiǎo shí	hours
旅行	lǚ xíng	vacation
看	kàn	to watch

	Pinyin	English Definition
球赛	qiú sài	sporting events

www.ingramcontent.com/pod-product-compliance
Lightning Source LLC
Chambersburg PA
CBHW041222070526
44584CB00001B/53